A Note to Parents

DK READERS is a compelling program for beginning readers, designed in conjunction with leading literacy experts, including Dr. Linda Gambrell, Director of the School of Education at Clemson University. Dr. Gambrell has served on the Board of Directors of the International Reading Association and as President of the National Reading Conference.

Beautiful illustrations and superb full-color photographs combine with engaging, easy-to-read stories to offer a fresh approach to each subject in the series. Each DK READER is guaranteed to capture a child's interest while developing his or her reading skills, general knowledge, and love of reading.

The four levels of DK READERS are aimed at different reading abilities, enabling you to choose the books that are exactly right for your child:

Level 1 – Beginning to read
Level 2 – Beginning to read alone
Level 3 – Reading alone
Level 4 – Proficient readers

The "normal" age at which a child begins to read can be anywhere from three to eight years old, so these levels are intended only as a general guideline.

No matter which level you select, you can be sure that you are helping your child learn to read, then read to learn!

LONDON, NEW YORK, MUNICH,
MELBOURNE, and DELHI

Publisher Neal Porter
Editor Andrea Curley
Art Editor Tina Vaughan

Produced by the
Shoreline Publishing Group
Editorial Director James Buckley, Jr.
Art Director Thomas J. Carling
Designer Helen Choy Whang
US Editor Regina Kahney
Reading Consultant
Linda Gambrell, Ph.D.

Produced in partnership and
licensed by Major League
Baseball Properties, Inc.
Executive Vice President Timothy J. Brosnan
Director of Publishing and MLB Photos
Don Hintze

First American Edition, 2001
06 10
Published in the United States by DK Publishing, Inc.
375 Hudson Street, New York, New York 10014

Published in Great Britain by Dorling Kindersley Limited.

ISBN: 0-1894-7341-0 (PLC)
ISBN: 0-7894-7340-2 (PB)

Library of Congress Cataloging-in-Publication Data
Buckley, James Jr.
  Home run heroes/by James Buckley, Jr.
    p. cm — (Dorling Kindersley readers)
  ISBN 0-7894-7341-0 — ISBN 0-7894-7340-2 (pbk.)
    1. Home runs (Baseball)—Juvenile literature. 2. Baseball players—
  Biography—Juvenile literature. [1. Home runs (Baseball) 2. Baseball
  players.] I. Title. II. Series

GV868.4 B83 2001
796.357′092′273—dc21
[B]
                                    00-055524

Color reproduction by Colourscan, Singapore.
Printed and bound in Mexico

Photography and illustration credits
All photos by Major League Baseball Photos except: **Andy Jurinko/Bill Goff,**
Inc. (illustrations): 26, 40; **Bill Purdom/Bill Goff, Inc.** (illustrations): 14, 42;
AP/Wide World: 4, 8, 22. **USC Trojan Athletics:** 32, 33.
All other images© Dorling Kindersley.
For further information see: www.dkimages.com

see our complete product line at

www.dk.com

Contents

DK READERS

READING
3
ALONE

BIG MAC, SAMMY & JUNIOR

HOME RUN HEROES

Written by James Buckley, Jr.

DK

DK Publishing, Inc.

Goin' yard

The most exciting play in baseball is a home run. A home run happens when the batter smashes the baseball out of the park! As the crowd screams for joy, the batter jogs around the bases. When he steps on home plate to score, he gets high-fives from his teammates.

Baseball players and fans have many nicknames for home runs. These include homer, dinger, tater, round-tripper, gopher ball, and "goin' yard." A home run that scores four runners is nicknamed a "grand salami." (It's really called a grand slam.)

But no matter what you call a home run, it's a special moment in any baseball game. New moments, and new memories, are created every day.

Three players creating memories today are among the greatest home run hitters ever!

Mark McGwire waves to the crowd after a big home run.

Ken Griffey, Jr., is called "the Kid" for his great attitude.

Ken Griffey, Jr., hit more home runs before the age of 30 than any other player in baseball history. "Junior" is one of the best all-around players in baseball history.

Sammy Sosa became the fourth player to hit 60 or more homers in one season, and is one of only two men to do that twice!

Mark McGwire set a new single-season home run record in 1998 by slugging an amazing 70 home runs! That broke a record that had stood for almost 30 years. In one incredible four-season stretch from 1996 to 1999, Mark blasted 248 home runs.

This book tells the stories of these three great Major League players... and how they became home run heroes.

Sammy Sosa is a slugger for the Chicago Cubs.

Junior's Jolts

Ken Griffey, Jr., was in the Major Leagues when he was less than 10 years old. He wasn't a player, of course. His dad, Ken Griffey, Sr., was an All-Star outfielder for the Cincinnati Reds and New York Yankees.

"Junior," as everyone called young Ken, loved to go to the ballpark with his dad. He learned to play from the many star players who were his dad's teammates.

"When the Reds won, the players' kids were allowed to go into the clubhouse," said Ken. A clubhouse is where players dress before and after a game.

"I guess that's why I like winning so much."

Junior learned to imitate the batting styles of the players. But over time, he developed his own sweet swing.

The little kid who followed his dad around the locker room has become one of the greatest players of all time.

In 1990, Junior and his dad boths played for Seattle.

Junior grew up
in Cincinnati, where
he was a star baseball
player in high school. He also
played basketball and football.

In 1987, the Seattle Mariners chose
Junior with the first pick in the amateur
baseball draft. He played less than two
seasons in the minor leagues before he
was ready for "The Show," which is
what some players call Major League
Baseball.

Junior's father was still playing
baseball when Junior made it.

All-Star Game
The All-Star Game is held
each summer. Players are
chosen by fans and coaches
to represent the American
and National Leagues.

In 1990, they became the first father and son in baseball history to play in the same outfield together. They even hit back-to-back home runs later that season! Junior was a slugger from the

The 1992 All-Star MVP

start. In 1991, only his third season, he had 100 runs batted in (RBI). In his career, he has had seven 100-RBI seasons! In 1992, Junior was the MVP of the All-Star Game.

Junior's home run swing improved as he got older. In 1993, he slugged 45 homers. In one stretch, he hit homers in eight games in a row, which tied a Major League record.

Junior was becoming a great all-around player, too, a good base-stealer, and one of the league's best outfielders. Junior has won 10 Gold Gloves, an award given to top fielders.

He also hits for a high average, with
seven .300 seasons to his credit.

As Junior improved, the Mariners
improved right along with him. Randy
Johnson, a tall lefthanded pitcher,
starred on the mound. Slugger Jay
Buhner played beside Junior in the
outfield. And Edgar Martinez was one of
the leagues' top hitters.

In 1995, thanks to all these great
players, the Mariners reached the
playoffs for the first time.

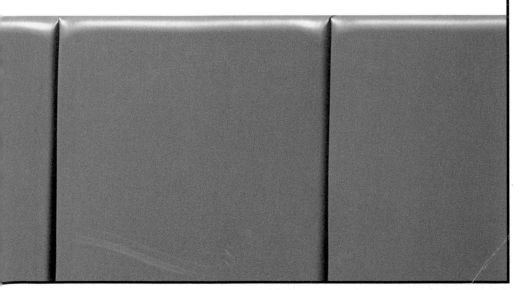

Seattle played the New York Yankees in the American League (A.L.) Division Series. Junior was the star, stroking five home runs in five games. The Mariners won the fifth and final game in the 11th inning, when Junior slid across the plate with the winning run.

After he scored, Junior leaped up and joined his teammates and their fans in a celebration.

Two years later, in 1997, Junior had one of his best seasons. The former clubhouse kid became the A.L. home run king, hitting an awesome 56 home runs and knocking in 147 runs.

Junior was named the A.L.'s Most Valuable Player.

The Mariners made the playoffs again after winning their first A.L. West championship.

With an unbroken streak of All-Star Game appearances, and more than 400 homers in his young career, Junior continued to be one of baseball's top stars.

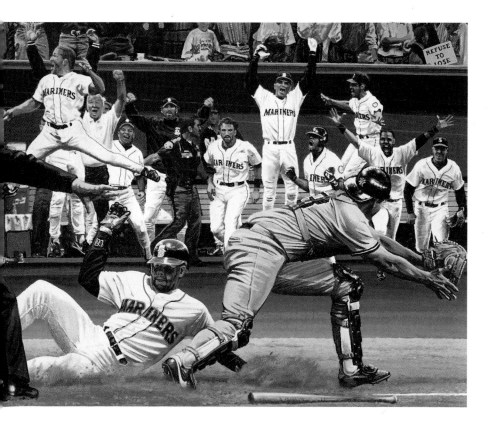

Junior hit 56 home runs in the 1998 season, and 48 in 1999.

At the All-Star Game in Boston in 1999, Major League Baseball named its "All-Century Team." Fans voted Junior as one of the top outfielders in baseball history...and he was only 29 years old!

After the 1999 season, Junior and the Mariners parted company. He missed his hometown of Cincinnati, and he had a chance to play there again.

Before the 2000 season, Junior signed with the Reds, his father's old team and the team he rooted for as a kid.

All Century Team

This special group of the 30 greatest baseball players of the 20th century was chosen in 1999.

He wore a big smile as he put on his new Reds jersey, with his father's old number 30 on the back.

"Every kid dreams about playing in his hometown," Junior said. "I'm excited to be home."

Junior is all smiles with the Reds.

For Junior, home is wherever he's playing Major League Baseball...and hitting home runs!

Slammin' Sammy

Until the 1998 season, Sammy Sosa was just another good baseball player from the Caribbean island of the Dominican Republic. Sammy had had a good career, including some fine seasons as a Chicago Cubs outfielder.

But in 1998, he burst into the headlines with a display of home run power that was like fireworks exploding!

Sammy joined Cardinals' first baseman Mark McGwire in a home run chase that thrilled the entire world, not just sports fans.

Throughout the summer, their head-to-head chase of the single-season record had all sports fans on the edge of their seats.

How did Sammy become a home run superstar? It all started in a dusty island town where baseball is king.

Dominican Republic
This Caribbean nation shares the island of Hispaniola with the nation of Haiti.

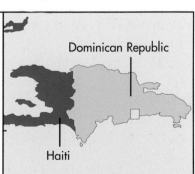

Sammy was born in a small town called San Pedro de Macoris [mock-uh-REES] in the Dominican Republic. The town was poor, but rich in baseball talent. More than a dozen Major League players have come from that one small town, including the players pictured here.

Tony Fernandez

Sammy and his friends played baseball in the streets. They didn't have fancy equipment; they used milk cartons for gloves, and tree

Miguel Tejada

branches or table legs for bats.

Baseballs were whatever sort of ball they could find.

On those streets Sammy developed the love and

passion for baseball that has helped him succeed.

"This game is all I have," Sammy said. "I give it every ounce of my energy."

Jose Offerman

Sammy took his energy to professional baseball when he was signed by the Texas Rangers in 1985. After playing in his first Major League game in April 1989, Sammy was traded to the Chicago White Sox in August 1989.

He's in there! Sammy scores for the White Sox.

He played with the White Sox for two years, adjusting to big-league pitching and continuing to learn the game.

In 1992, he was traded again, this time to the Chicago Cubs.

Sammy quickly became a star in the National League. He combined a powerful bat with great speed. In 1993, he joined the elite "30-30 Club." This means he had more than 30 homers (33) and 30 steals (36) in one season. He was the first player in Cubs history to accomplish this feat. Then he did it again in 1995, hitting 36 homers and stealing 34 bases.

Sammy became a Cub.

Sammy also had a cannon for an arm, and baserunners learned not to challenge him.

Over the next few seasons, Sammy kept improving his home run swing.

Sammy had 35 or more homers in 1995, 1996, and 1997. But that was just a warm-up for what was to come.

Through the first two months of the 1998 season, Sammy had 13 home runs. Mark McGwire had 27.

But suddenly, in June of 1998, Sammy started a huge power surge. In that month, he powered 20 home runs, a Major League record for one month.

The Great Home Run Race was on!

Sammy does his home run hop...then points to the sky.

The homers flew out of ballparks across the country. Sammy slugged one, then Mark pounded one.

Each time Sammy hit another homer, he dropped his bat and did a big two-footed hop out on his way to first base. After he finished rounding the bases, he touched his heart and then blew a kiss. Sammy said that this was his way to remember his mother and his family supporting him back home in the Dominican Republic.

Finally, on September 8, Mark McGwire broke the single-season record of 61, held by Roger Maris. Sammy's Cubs were playing Mark's Cardinals. Sammy sprinted in from the outfield to congratulate his home run opponent.

Sammy's sportsmanlike joy made him more of a hero than his powerful bat. Sammy was a good sport because he showed respect for Mark.

Then, just a week after Mark broke the magic mark of 61, Sammy hit his 62nd, too!

What was more important to Sammy as a member of the Cubs was that his homer heroics helped Chicago earn its first playoff spot since the 1985 season.

Sammy ended the season with an amazing 66 home runs and a Major League-leading 158 RBI. He was named the N.L. Most Valuable Player.

Some people think that Sammy and Mark's home run chase – and the positive way they approached it – helped make baseball popular again. Fans around the world became interested in the game again.

Sammy was popular around the world. He and some other Major Leaguers traveled to Japan after the 1998 season.

To prove that he was no one-season wonder, Sammy hit another 63 home runs in 1999. Sammy and Mark McGwire are the

Baseball in Japan

Baseball has been played in Japan since the early 1900s. A popular pro league there has 12 teams.

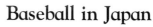

only players
in baseball
history who
have more
than one

Sammy's smile lit up Japan.

season of 60 homers.
Sammy's enthusiasm
for baseball and his
dedication to
excellence have
taken him a long
way...all the way
from his home in
the Dominican
Republic to a
place in the
baseball record
books!

*The sweet swing of a
home run king!*

Big Mac

When big Mark McGwire strides to the plate, everyone expects the ball to end up in one place: the outfield seats!

Mark set the baseball world on fire with a tremendous home run binge from 1996-1999. In each of those four seasons, he hit more than 50 home runs. No one has ever had a streak like that.

In 1998, he broke the single-season record when he clubbed 70 homers, breaking the old record by nine!

Since he set a rookie home run record in 1987, Mark has become one of baseball's best home run hitters. His powerful arms and quick wrists send pitches flying into the sky.

With more than 500 home runs, he is in baseball's all-time top 10, and still going strong.

Mark not only is a home run hitter, he hits for a good average, too. His story has captured the hearts of Americans, whether they are baseball fans or not.

Big Mac is six feet, five inches tall and weighs 225 pounds.

Believe it or not, Big Mac started his baseball career as a pitcher. In Little League, he once went three seasons without losing.

Mark was also great at golf. He became so good that he quit playing baseball for a year during high school.

McGwire as a Trojan

But soon he returned to the diamond. He continued to star on the mound, but he was also developing as a slugger.

Mark earned a baseball scholarship to the University of Southern California (USC), where he pitched and played first base as a freshman.

He concentrated on hitting the next season, and wound up setting a school record for home runs! Mark's career as a pitcher was over...and his life as a home run slugger was just beginning.

Big Mac as a USC slugger

At USC, Mark kept "goin' yard." Along with helping Team USA in the Pan Am Games, Mark set a USC career record with 54 home runs in just three seasons at USC.

The former golfer was ready for the Major Leagues.

The Oakland Athletics chose Mark in the first round of the 1984 draft.

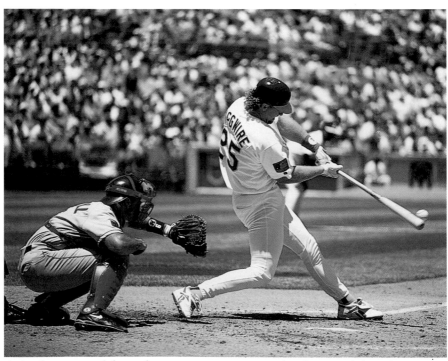

Mark started his slugging career with the Oakland A's.

Olympics
This international sports competition is held every four years. Baseball has been an Olympic medal sport since 1992.

After competing for his country again at the Summer Olympics, where Mark helped the team win a silver medal, he began playing pro baseball.

He played two seasons in the minor league, and made "the Show" in 1987 as Oakland's starting first baseman. Mark wasted no time in making his mark. In May, just his second month in the Majors, he slugged 15 homers, just one short of the all-time record!

Big Mac ended 1987 with 49 home runs, the most ever by a rookie (a player in his first season).

The next season, Oakland won its first American League championship since 1974. In 1989, the A's won the A.L. again. This time, though, they also won the World Series! Oakland defeated the San Francisco Giants in four games.

In 1990, Mark had 39 homers as the A's again won the A.L. title, only to lose to Cincinnati in the World Series.

Each year from 1987 to 1992, Mark was selected to the A.L. All-Star team.

Mark was a great home run hitter on a top team, but he was not an all-time great...yet.

And when he missed most of the 1993 and 1994 seasons with injuries, it seemed as if his career might come to a sudden stop.

But Mark was as tough mentally as he was strong physically.

He battled back from injuries to his foot and in 1996 bashed 52 home runs,

the most in his career to that point.

Big Mac was back!

In 1997, however, Big Mac took his act—and his big bat—to a new town.

In Oakland, Mark and Jose Canseco were called the "Bash Brothers."

By the middle of the 1997 season, Mark and the Athletics knew that their future together was short. Oakland probably couldn't pay him what he was worth, so they traded him to St. Louis.

The Cardinals got a bargain. Big Mac had a total of 58 home runs in 1997, including 24 in the 51 games Mark played for St. Louis.

Roger Maris

This Yankees' outfielder hit 61 home runs in 1961 to break Babe Ruth's mark of 60. Maris won two MVP awards in his career.

Excited about his success in his new home city, Mark signed with the Cardinals for 1998 and beyond.

And beyond is just where he went in 1998. It was his best season ever!

Yankees outfielder Roger Maris held the single-season home run record of 61. Many people thought it would never be broken. But as 1998 began, many baseball fans and players began to think that "never" had arrived.

Mark started his race for the record in style, clubbing a grand slam on Opening Day.

By the end of May, 1998, Mark had 27 home runs. The race to 61 was on! Every day, fans around the world waited for news of Big Mac's at-bats.

Did he go yard again today? How far did he slug it? How many does he need?

Big Mac swings into history with his 62nd home run.

When Sammy Sosa slugged a record 20 home runs in June, suddenly it was a two-man race. Back and forth the two superstars went, matching each other homer for homer.

In July, Mark's 45th home run broke a 58-year-old Cardinals team record. But that wasn't the record he was aiming for.

He reached 50 home runs in August, the fourth season in a row he had reached that total.

Finally, on September 8, with the whole sports world watching, he did it.

Mark McGwire slammed a pitch from Chicago's Steve Trachsel into the left-field seats for his 62nd home run.

Big Mac had broken the unbreakable home run record!

The fans in the stadium went wild. Mark's teammates streamed out of the dugout to congratulate him. Sammy Sosa, playing right field that night for Chicago, sprinted in to congratulate his home run rival.

One special fan, Mark's son, Matt, helped lead the cheers. He was working as a bat boy, so he got an up-close and personal look at history.

In the stands, Roger Maris' family stood and cheered, too. Mark has chased their father's record with class and dignity. They were proud that a great guy had broken their dad's record.

But the drama of 1998 continued ever after Mark broke the record. Sammy Sosa reached 62 homers only five days later.

Throughout September, the pair traded the home run record lead back and forth. Going into the final weekend of the season, both players had 66 home runs.

Who would come out on top?

After No. 62, Big Mac gave his son a bear hug.

Mark answered that question quickly. On Saturday of the final weekend, he slugged two homers. On Sunday, he slammed two more. Big Mac ended the season with an amazing *70 home runs*!

The home run battle between Mark and Sammy helped make 1998 one of the most memorable baseball seasons of all time.

Mark added more memories to the baseball scrapbook in 1999 by hitting 68 more home runs. Sammy added 63 to continue their head-to-head battle.

The homers just kept on coming!

Hammerin' Hank
Hank Aaron holds the all-time career home run record with 755. Can Mark capture that record someday, too?

Mark McGwire, Sammy Sosa, and Ken Griffey, Jr., continue to slug home runs. But is there a young player somewhere who will grow up to break their records?

Keep swinging...it might be *you*!

The Big Three

Here are the home run records of Ken Griffey, Jr., Sammy Sosa, and Mark McGwire through the 1999 season. You can add their totals from future seasons in the spaces provided.

Mark McGwire

YEAR	HOME RUNS	YEAR	HOME RUNS
1986	3	1994	9
1987	49	1995	39
1988	32	1996	52
1989	33	1997	58
1990	39	1998	70
1991	22	1999	66
1992	42	2000	___
1993	9	2001	___

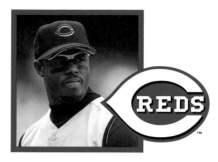

Sammy Sosa

Ken Griffey, Jr.

YEAR	HOME RUNS
1989	4
1990	15
1991	10
1992	8
1993	33
1994	25
1995	36
1996	40
1997	36
1998	66
1999	63
2000	____
2001	____

YEAR	HOME RUNS
1989	16
1990	22
1991	22
1992	27
1993	45
1994	40
1995	17
1996	49
1997	56
1998	56
1999	48
2000	____
2001	____

Glossary

Clubhouse
The baseball term for the locker room where players dress before and after a game. It is also the place players hold meetings, hang out, or eat meals.

Draft
An annual meeting of pro sports clubs at which they choose players, usually from colleges or high schools, to join their teams.

Freshman
A person in his or her first year of college or high school.

Grand slam
A home run hit with the bases loaded; it scores four runs.

Minor leagues
Pro baseball organizations that are not part of the Major Leagues.

Opening Day
The special name given to the first day of the season.

Pan Am Games
An international athletic competition held every four years among the nations of North, Central, and South America.

Scholarship
An award of college fees given to students for academic or athletic feats.

Sportsmanlike
Acting like a "good sport" means being positive about your performance and your opponent no matter whether you win or lose.

Stolen base
When a baserunner runs from one base to another while the pitcher throws.

Streak
In sports, a streak is any series of games or moments that add up to a great feat. For instance, a "hitting streak" means getting at least one hit in any number of games in a row.

World Series
Major League Baseball's annual championship series, held in late October between the champions of the American and National Leagues.